The Marc Brown Connection

by Will C. Howell

FEARON TEACHER AIDS

Simon & Schuster Supplementary Education Group

Marc Brown,

Webster says a doctor is "one skilled in the healing arts." I think that your parents got their wish. Through the integrity, courage, and humor in your books, you have provided hope, consolation, and laughter (the best medicine) for millions of readers. You are most definitely skilled in the healing arts.

Will Howell

Editor: Carol Williams
Copyeditor: Kristin Eclov
Illustration: Gwen Connelly
Cover illustration: Reprinted from *Arthur's Baby* with the permission of
    Marc Brown.
Design: Diann Abbott

ISBN 0-8224-4378-3

Printed in the United States of America
1. 9 8 7 6 5 4 3 2 1

Contents

Introduction

The emphasis on "The Year of the Young Reader" (1989) and "International Literacy Year" (1990) has helped children's literature come of age. Research confirms that good reading and writing are best taught by using good books. And today, educators are fortunate to have a wide selection of excellent children's books to choose from.

The Marc Brown Connection is written for librarians and teachers who want to effectively use good literature in their classrooms. The lessons present art, math, creative writing, science, and social studies activities to accompany books written and illustrated by this one outstanding author. The variety of interdisciplinary activities and the whole-language instructional approach incorporated in the lessons will help you meet the diverse needs and interests of your students.

As students become familiar with various works by a single author, they develop an ability to analyze literary and artistic style. Children can go to the library and select books written or illustrated by authors they feel as if they have actually met. "Connecting" with authors stimulates students to become involved in and enthusiastic about reading, writing, and learning. *The Marc Brown Connection* gives students the opportunity to meet an author/illustrator who has established himself in the field of children's literature.

Lessons require minimal preparation, while resulting in maximum participation and learning. A brief synopsis of each book is included. Read the book aloud to the children and invite them to enjoy the illustrations before participating in the activities. Activities such as making swimsuits, designing glasses, and creating pop-up books will help you to enhance and reinforce your curriculum.

Meet Marc Brown

Marc Brown was born on November 25, 1946, in Erie, Pennsylvania. With his three sisters, Marc grew up listening to stories told by his grandmother, Thora. Later, he was to carry on the tradition of telling stories to his own children, Tolon, Tucker, and Eliza, the inspiration for the story *Arthur's Baby*. It was a story that Marc told his son, Tolon, that led to his first book, *Arthur's Nose*.

Marc Brown draws on his own colorful experiences and feelings to create books that are both realistic and sensitive. Marc tried out many jobs before finding his place as a well-loved children's book author. He made deliveries for a florist, but kept getting lost. He worked as a soda jerk, but continually confused the cook with the language he used to place his orders. Marc had the lead in a summer stock theater production of "Bye, Bye, Birdy," but lost that job because he couldn't sing. He was a college professor at a well-established 103-year-old college until it closed during his term of employment.

Marc has since found his way into children's books. He has given us language we can enjoy, created his own kind of music, and taken creative liberties that have resulted in strong and individual books. As for his stint as a college professor, Marc is still teaching through his wonderful stories.

In 1980, Marc Brown won the Boston Globe Horn Book Award for illustration. His Arthur series continues to be a favorite among children. In fact, the Arthur character is so popular, a fan club has been organized. Students can find out more about the Arthur Fan Club by writing to:

Little, Brown and Company
34 Beacon Street
Boston, Massachusetts 02108-1493

Marc and his wife, Laurene Krasny Brown, have collaborated on books about television production, art museums, baby care, and divorce. Their careful research and humorous style have made their books very readable and helpful to parents and children alike. Today, the Browns live in a 350-year-old house in Hingham, Massachusetts.

Arthur Goes

Arthur's father may have fond memories of his camp days, but Arthur experiences homesickness, bad food, and camp competitions. Arthur decides to run away from camp, until the big scavenger hunt with Camp Horsewater creates an interesting turn of events.

Boston: Little, Brown, 1982

to Camp

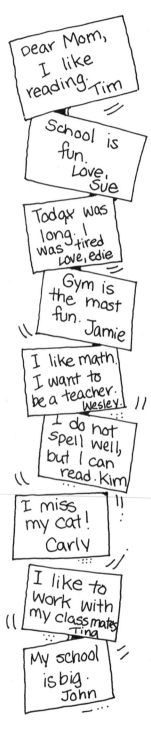

Materials:

- 3" x 5" ruled index cards
- pencils

Lesson Procedure

1. After reading the entire book aloud to the class, reread the postcards that Arthur wrote to his family. Discuss Arthur's feelings about camp.
2. Give each student five or six ruled index cards.
3. Encourage students to practice their writing skills by expressing their feelings about school. Invite the students to use one index card to write a postcard message to their parents explaining their feelings about school.
4. Send the postcards home with the students at the end of the day.
5. This activity could be stretched out over a period of one week. Students could write a postcard message at the end of each day.

Taking It Further . . .

Organize your classroom around a camp theme for one entire day. Design activities using camp jargon, such as target practice (math), camp grub (nutrition), and scavenger hunt (language arts). Organize the class into teams. Before "camp day," send a letter home to parents explaining the day's theme and that they should expect "letters" from their "campers." At the end of the day, invite students to write a letter home to their parents explaining the day's events and their reactions and feelings.

❧ • MAPPING • ❧

Materials:

- 12" x 18" drawing paper
- pencils
- colored pencils, crayons, or markers (optional)

Lesson Procedure

1. Show children the endpapers of the book so they can get a closer look at the layout of Camp Meadowcroak.
2. Ask children to name the places they see on the map and make a list of these places on the chalkboard.

boys' tent	nurse	swim pond
girls' tent	campfire	mess hall
main lodge	archery range	

3. Give each student a 12" x 18" sheet of drawing paper to design their own camp map. Encourage students to include at least ten places or features and to label each place or provide a legend explaining map symbols.
4. After completing the maps, students can color them with colored pencils, crayons, or markers.

Taking It Further . . .

Children can design advertising brochures explaining the highlights of their fictitious camps.

❧ CURRICULUM SCAVENGER HUNT ❧

Materials:

- lined paper
- pencils
- textbooks or encyclopedias

Lesson Procedure

1. Discuss the scavenger hunt that Arthur and his fellow campers embarked on by reviewing the list of items they were instructed to find.

frog	sunglasses	banana	flashlight
oak leaf	sneaker	alarm clock	
balloon			

2. Divide the class into teams of 4-6 students.

3. Choose an area of the curriculum, such as math, language arts, or social studies, and compose a list of items for students to find. Some sample lists might include:

Math	Language Arts	Social Studies
something 2 $\frac{1}{2}$ inches long	an irregular past tense verb	a country in Africa
a rectangle	a simile	a famous pioneer
a 45° angle	a metaphor	a country that grows wheat
the product of 6 x 7	a synonym for *big*	

4. Give teams a time limit to locate or think of as many of the items on the list as they can. Team members can use textbooks and encyclopedias to help find the information, but they must also identify their sources.

Taking It Further . . .

Encourage students to write scavenger-hunt lists as an evaluation of a book they have read or as a review of a curriculum unit. For example, a student might write the following list of things to find after reading the book:

a nervous camper	a mean counselor	a fake bear
a nice counselor	cookies	a happy camper

Arthur's

It's the end of March and everyone is thinking about April Fool's Day, except Arthur. Arthur is thinking about being pulverized by the school bully, Binky Barnes. The story is full of tricks and surprises, but Arthur's trick on Binky is the best trick of all.

A·P·R·I·L
1

Boston: Little, Brown, 1983

April Fool

CREATIVE WRITING

Materials:

•worksheet on page 13
•pencils

Lesson Procedure

1. Remind students of Arthur's magic telescope that "lets you see things you've never seen before." Ask students what they would like to be able to see if they had a chance to look into the magic telescope.
2. Give each student a worksheet to describe what they would like to see through a magic telescope. Remind students that Arthur told Binky Barnes he would only be able to see through the telescope if he knew the secret words. Invite students to include an explanation of what makes their magic telescopes work.

Taking It Further . . .

Ask students to recall some of the April Fool's tricks that Arthur's classmates played on one another (the endpapers of the book contain an illustrated collection of the tricks). Students can write step-by-step directions for an original trick.

Name _____

What Can You See with My Magic Telescope?

The Marc Brown Connection © 1991 Fearon Teacher Aids

❧ • RELATIONSHIPS • ❧

Materials:

Lesson Procedure

1. Remind students how D.W. "barged into Arthur's room." Arthur was offended by this invasion of his privacy. Ask students to name some other ways that a person's privacy can be invaded.

   violation of a person's space (standing or sitting too close)
   intruding into a person's personal thoughts (reading a diary)
   sharing confidential information (gossiping)

2. Ask students to name some places that are private. They might name the bedroom, a tree, a fort, a basement, or an attic.
3. Privacy can be difficult to maintain. Discuss how students can help provide privacy for themselves and others at home or in the classroom.

   Determine a family sign or signal to use at home when one wants to be alone.
   Use music or literature to create a private world in the classroom.
   Provide isolated study carrels in the classroom.

4. Discuss ways to respect others' need for privacy.

Taking It Further . . .

Your Own Secret Place by Byrd Baylor (New York: Scribner's, 1979) is another good book that deals with privacy. Recommend that students find this book in the library.

❧ • SHADOW ART • ☙

Materials:

- drawing paper
- large sheet of butcher paper
- black crayons
- pencils
- spotlight, lamp, or overhead projector

Lesson Procedure

1. Remind students of the shadow tricks Francine and Muffy did in the story. Ask students if they have ever tried to make shadow pictures.
2. Tape the large sheet of butcher paper on a wall and shine a bright light on it. Invite children to experiment with shadow tricks by standing in front of the light and positioning their hands in various ways to cast shadows on the butcher paper.
3. When each student has developed a shadow trick, have a partner trace the shadow picture onto the butcher paper. Label each shadow picture with the designer's name.
4. After the paper is filled with shadow drawings, children can color the drawings in with black crayon.

Taking It Further . . .

Encourage students to make shadow drawings on colored construction paper and then cut the designs out for display on a bulletin board.

Arthur's

Arthur gets unsolicited advice from his friends and is heckled by his sister when the announcement is made of the arrival of a new baby at Arthur's house. D.W. insists that Arthur "doesn't know beans about babies." In the end, Arthur proves he has everything under control.

Boston: Little, Brown, 1987

Baby

• MATH •

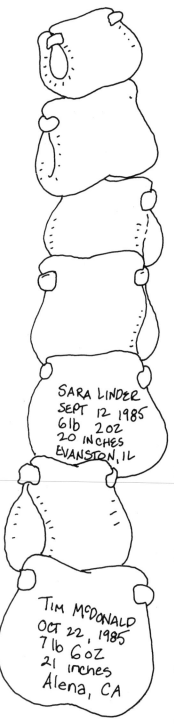

Materials:

- paper diapers
- markers

Lesson Procedure

1. Give each student a paper diaper. Ask students to use a marker to write the following information on their diapers: full name, birth date, hospital where born, city and state, weight at birth, and length at birth. (If students do not know all the information, have them take the diapers home and ask their parents to help them complete the project.)

   Arthur's baby sister's diaper, for example, would have the following information written on it.

Kate	Boston, Massachusetts
September, 1987	7 lb. 6 oz.
Beth Israel Hospital	20 inches

2. Use the information on the diapers to make charts, graphs, or tables. For example, make a graph comparing weights or lengths. Or, make a bar graph showing how many students were born in each month of the year.

3. Use the data to draw conclusions and make predictions.

   How much does an average baby weigh?
   In what month might most babies be born this year?

Taking It Further . . .

Display a large map on a bulletin board. Use push pins to locate the city and state where each student was born.

Arthur's

Arthur invites all of his friends to his birthday party. Muffy is having a party on the same day and has invited the same friends. The situation becomes a stand-off between the girls and the boys, until Arthur comes up with a plan to save the day for everyone.

Boston: Little, Brown, 1989

Birthday

❧ WRITING INVITATIONS ❧

Materials:

- lined paper
- 9" x 12" construction paper
- crayons or markers
- glue
- pencils

Lesson Procedure

1. Plan to have a class birthday party to celebrate everyone's birthday at the same time. (If you are really ambitious, you could have a special party each month for all the children who have a birthday in that month.)
2. Discuss the important information that should be included on a party invitation.

   Who the party is for.
   What the guests should bring.
   Where the party takes place.

   Why the celebration is being planned.
   When the party takes place, including the day, date, and time.

3. Write each child's name on a slip of paper and put the names in a bag. Have each student draw a name out of the bag.
4. Have each child create a party invitation addressed to the person whose name they drew, inviting them to the all-student class birthday party.
5. Encourage the students to use correct letter form to write the invitation information on lined paper.
6. Have students glue the letter on the colored construction paper and then fold the paper in half.
7. Students can decorate the outside of the folded invitation.

Taking It Further . . .

Divide the class into several groups of 4-6 students to plan games, decorations, refreshments, and clean up. To make the clean-up crew seem more appealing, invite those who clean up to remain after the party is over and take home all the party leftovers!

Arthur's Birthday

❧• CALCULATING TIME •❧

Materials:

• lined paper
• pencils

Lesson Procedure

1. Ask students to recall activities that were a part of Arthur's birthday party. Make a list of the activities on the chalkboard.
2. As a class, decide on an amount of time that would be needed to do each activity.

   hiding and waiting for Muffy to arrive—10 minutes
   blowing out the candles and eating cake—20 minutes
   opening presents—20 minutes
   playing spin the bottle—30 minutes
   cleaning up—60 minutes

3. Give each child a sheet of lined paper. Encourage students to make a time schedule for Arthur's party based on the activities and time allotments already discussed. Explain to students that the invitations said that the party was to begin at 2:00 and to begin their schedules from that time.

   2:00 p.m. party begins (hide and wait for Muffy)
   2:10 p.m. blow out candles and eat cake
   2:30 p.m. open presents
   2:50 p.m. play spin the bottle
   3:20 p.m. party ends
   4:20 p.m. clean-up is finished

Taking It Further . . .

Invite students to plan a schedule for a class party.

Arthur's

Only two more days until Christmas and Arthur cannot decide what to give Santa. D.W. cannot decide what else to add to her list. Arthur's present for Santa surprises everyone and D.W. has a surprise for Arthur.

Boston: Little, Brown, 1984

Christmas

❧ • FUN WITH WORDS • ❧

Materials:

•lined paper
•pencils

Lesson Procedure

1. Marc Brown has fun with language when he writes. Ask students if they noticed some unusual or amusing word choices.

   D.W. said she "teached" Killer a trick.
   Ice cream flavors, such as "bumpy road," "ant sherbert," "frog chip," and "bat wing."
   A catalog called "Spears Wish Book."
   The waitress yelling, "Catch a fish, hit it with rye, and put a pair of shoes on it" when placing Santa's order.

2. Have students write an interesting sentence using a play on words. Or encourage students to illustrate figures of speech that would be misunderstood if taken literally.

3. Read aloud other stories that present some interesting and amusing word choices and misunderstandings.

   Day, Alexander. *Frank and Ernest*. New York: Scholastic, 1988.
   Gwynne, Fred. *Chocolate Moose for Dinner*. New York: Prentice-Hall, 1987.
   Parish, Peggy. *Amelia Bedelia*. New York: Harper, 1963.
   Wiseman, Bernard. *Morris the Moose*. New York: Scholastic, 1977.

Taking It Further . . .

Ask students why they think Arthur's family named their dog "Killer." Take another look at the illustrations of the dog and ask students if they think the name is appropriate. Invite students to share names they have given their pets and ask them to explain why they chose the name they did. Ask students to share stories about why their parents named them as they did. Use a book of names to look up each student's name and tell its meaning and origin.

Arthur's Christmas

✦ ADDING MONEY ✦

Materials:

- lined paper
- pencils
- catalogs or sales tabloids
- calculators (optional)

Lesson Procedure

1. Discuss how Arthur was working within a limited budget to do his Christmas shopping. Point out the page in the book that shows Arthur looking through "Spears Wish Book" catalog.
2. Hand out catalogs or sales tabloids. (Most department stores are very cooperative in donating sales tabloids, especially toward the end of a sale.)
3. Explain to the students that they should pretend they each have $50.00 to buy gifts for their family and friends. Invite students to look through the sales catalogs and make a list of the items they would purchase. Have students write the amount each purchase would cost beside the items. Students can total their purchases and try to come as close to the $50.00 limit as possible.
4. Try the same activity, but increase the budget to $100.00 and have students use calculators to figure their totals.

Taking It Further . . .

Have students make their own personal wish lists before handing out catalogs. Then have students use the catalogs to calculate the total cost of the items on their wish lists. They may be surprised at the total price. Or, have students make a list of gifts they can give or receive that do not cost any money (doing a chore for someone, writing a poem, playing a game together).

Arthur's

Arthur can't read the math problems on the chalkboard or make a basket during basketball practice. After visiting the optometrist, Arthur has a new problem—his friends tease him about the way he looks in his new glasses. At first, Arthur tries to hide his glasses, but eventually finds a better solution to his problem.

Boston: Little, Brown, 1979

Eyes

☙ • BOOK REPORT • ❧

Materials:

•drawing paper
•lined paper
•pencils
•magazines

Lesson Procedure

1. After reading the story aloud, look at the illustrations again with the students and ask them to notice the various types of glasses worn by different characters in the book. Discuss how the style of the glasses fits each character or tells something about his or her personality.
2. Encourage students to look through magazines to find pictures of other types of glasses.
3. Invite students to design a pair of glasses for a character in a book they have read. On the lined paper, have students write the title of the book they have read and the character's name. Have students then explain why they designed the glasses they did for that character. Encourage students to include information about the character's personality to justify their design.

Taking It Further . . .

Without showing the titles of the books or the characters' names, display the glasses and explanations for the designs. In a separate area, display the book titles and character names. Invite students to match the glasses with the appropriate characters.

Arthur's Eyes

Materials:

- •worksheet on page 30
- •pencils
- •multicultural stories, picture books, or novels
- •informational books about different cultures

Lesson Procedure

1. In the story, glasses helped Arthur see things more clearly. Discuss the meaning of the phrase, "Looking at the world through rose-colored glasses." Explain that we often do not see or understand things clearly or as they really are because we sometimes are unaware of things that are happening in the world around us.
2. Help students get a clearer picture of the world they live in by reading some stories that explain cultures and traditions that are different from their own.
3. Using the worksheet on page 30, have students write facts and insights they have gained about another culture.

Taking It Further . . .

Francine liked to wear "movie star" glasses. Discuss famous people who wear glasses. Cut pictures from magazines showing people wearing glasses. Use the pictures to make a collage of glasses on a bulletin board.

Name _____

The Way I See It in

_____
(name of culture)

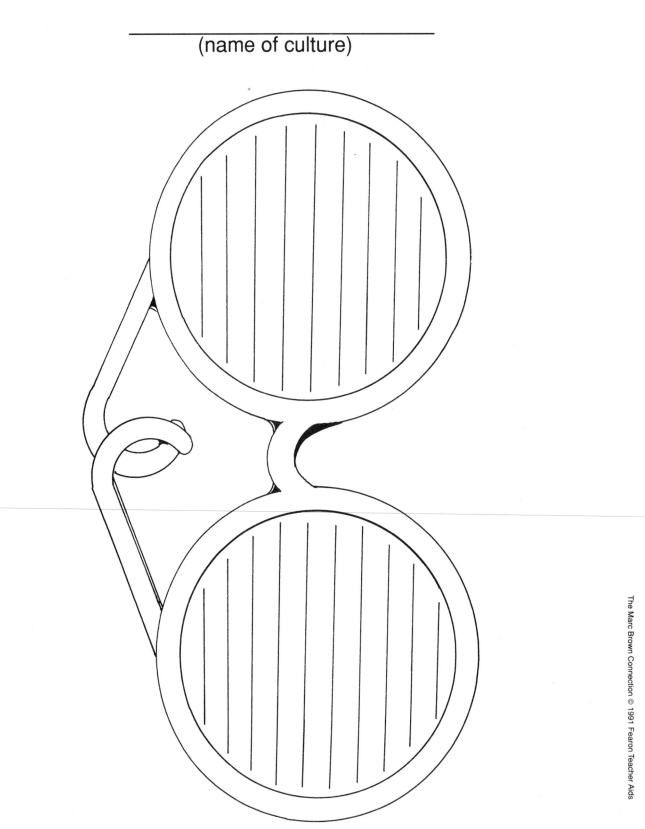

Arthur's Eyes

❧• ART •❧

Materials:

- •assorted colors of construction paper
- •a variety of materials, such as pipe cleaners, wire, straws, popsicle sticks, glitter, and beads
- •glue
- •scissors

Lesson Procedure

1. Remind students how Arthur tried on all kinds of frames before he chose the ones he liked best.
2. Invite students to use the supply of materials you have provided to design some new frames for Arthur. Encourage creativity and originality.

Taking It Further . . .

After students have designed new glasses for Arthur, have them pretend that the glasses are magic. Ask students to write a story about the glasses, answering these questions: What will the glasses do? How will they work? What trouble might they cause?

Arthur's

Arthur is embarrassed about his aardvark nose. It gets red when he has a cold and gets in the way when he tries to play hide-and-seek. Arthur decides it is time for a change.

Boston: Little, Brown, 1976

Nose

Materials:

Lesson Procedure

1. Make a list on the chalkboard of the elements of a good story.

> Plot—action with a definite beginning, middle, and end. A problem should be presented in the beginning, struggled with in the middle, and resolved in the end.
> Characters—hero (protagonist) and villain (antagonist).
> Style—the way a story is told (words and pictures).
> Setting—where and when the story takes place.
> Theme—the message of the story (friendship, courage, and so on).

2. Discuss these elements as they relate to the story.

> Plot—Arthur is embarrassed by his big nose (beginning).
> His friends make fun of his nose so Arthur decides to change it (middle). Arthur decides to keep his nose. His friends accept him as he is. There is more to Arthur than his nose (end).
> Characters—Arthur, the hero, is gentle and sensitive.
> Francine is a bit of an antagonist with her abrasiveness.
> Style—Marc Brown calls on children's common experiences and presents them with humor in his writing and illustrations.
> Setting—Children will easily identify with the everyday setting.
> Theme—The theme could be self-acceptance, seeing the whole person, or appreciating the differences in people.

Taking It Further . . .

Arthur tried to change the way he looked. Students can temporarily change their outer appearances by making masks. Younger children can make paper-plate animal masks. Older students can make celebrity masks accenting special features of famous athletes, actors, or political leaders.

❧ • SELF-AWARENESS • ❧

Materials:

- •worksheet on page 36
- •crayons or markers
- •photograph of each student

Lesson Procedure

1. Point out the family pictures on the book jacket and in the illustrations throughout the book.
2. Feature a "Student of the Week" in your classroom by preparing a special display on a bulletin board.
3. Give each student a copy of the picture frame worksheet to color and decorate. Have each student glue a photograph of themselves in the center of the frame.
4. Display one student-made picture frame each week. Add additional family pictures, the jacket of the student's favorite book, a favorite poem, or anything else the student would like to display that helps classmates get to know him or her better.

Taking It Further . . .

Students can draw a picture of themselves rather than gluing a photograph inside the picture frame. Invite children to fill the surrounding space with descriptive words about themselves.

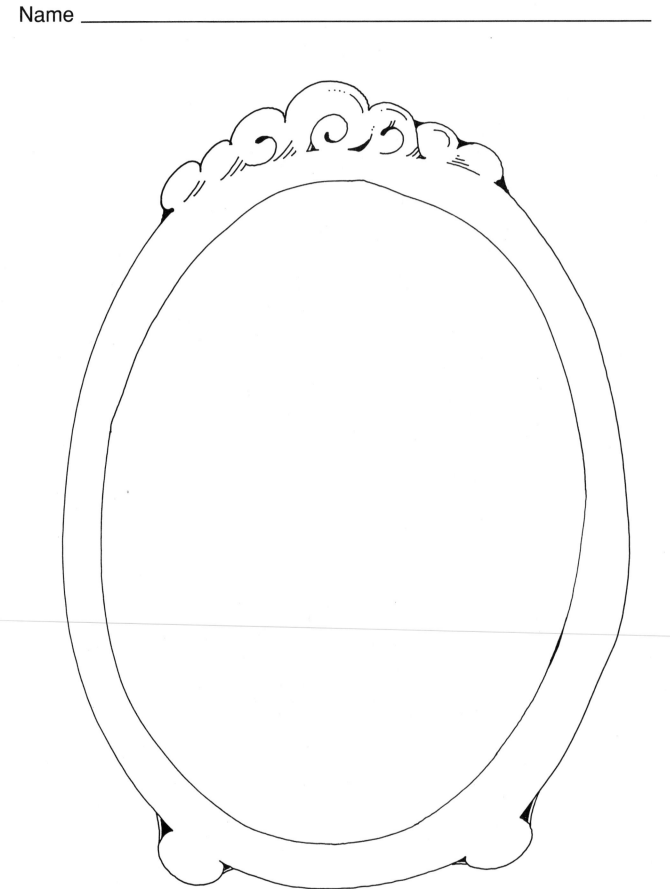

Arthur's Nose

Arthur's

On the first day of third grade, Arthur gets Mr. Ratburn (also known as the "Rat") as his teacher. Along with that comes homework and one hundred spelling words. When Arthur is chosen to be in the school spellathon, he wonders whether he can possibly accomplish all that is expected of him. The day of the spellathon is filled with excitement and surprises, including an unexpected announcement made by Mr. Ratburn.

Boston: Little, Brown, 1986

Teacher Trouble

❧ CREATIVE WRITING ❧

Materials:

•drawing paper
•pencils

Lesson Procedure

1. Discuss how the students in the story evaluated Mr. Ratburn.

   "I can't believe he gave us homework the first day."
   "Make one wrong move and he puts you on death row."
   "He's really a vampire with magical powers."
   "I got the strictest teacher in the whole world."

2. In contrast with Mr. Ratburn's reputation, Miss Sweetwater made popcorn for her class and Mrs. Fink took her class on a field trip to the aquarium. Ask students for their thoughts on what makes an ideal teacher.

3. Have students draw a picture of the ideal teacher. Invite students to write complete sentences to label special features and attitudes of their ideal teachers.

   Only soft words come from his mouth.
   She has a brain that just won't quit. She knows everything.
   She holds your hand when you are alone.
   His heart is big enough for twenty-five kids.

Taking It Further . . .

Have students compare Mr. Ratburn with Miss Viola Swamp in Harry Allard's *Miss Nelson Is Missing*.

Arthur's

Arthur soon finds out that being director of the school play is not all glamour and glory. When everyone refuses to play the part of the turkey, Arthur must make some last minute changes.

Boston: Little, Brown, 1983

Thanksgiving

Materials:

- paper plates
- paper cups
- glue
- scissors
- tape
- stapler
- crayons or markers

Lesson Procedure

1. Give each student a paper plate and one paper cup. Make available glue, scissors, tape, stapler, and markers or crayons.
2. Invite students to create their own unique turkeys using the available materials. Do not give students specific directions. Encourage them to use their imaginations and be creative. Hopefully, you will end up with as many different types of turkeys as there are students in the class.

Taking It Further . . .

Arthur had trouble recruiting his classmates to play the all-important role of the turkey in the school play. Invite students to write a persuasive paragraph telling why they should *not* have to play the turkey in the school Thanksgiving play.

Arthur's Thanksgiving

Arthur's

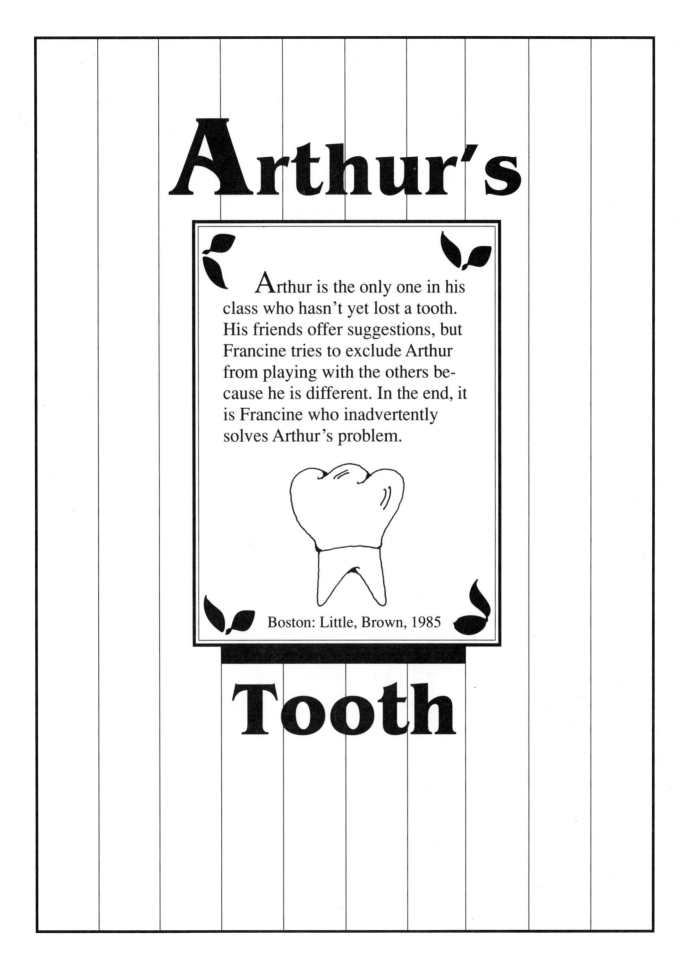

Arthur is the only one in his class who hasn't yet lost a tooth. His friends offer suggestions, but Francine tries to exclude Arthur from playing with the others because he is different. In the end, it is Francine who inadvertently solves Arthur's problem.

Boston: Little, Brown, 1985

Tooth

CREATIVE WRITING

Materials:

- •worksheet on page 43
- •pencils

Lesson Procedure

1. Discuss the ways in which Arthur's friends tried to help him.

   Buster brought carrots for Arthur's lunch.
   Sue Ellen showed Arthur how to put raisins over his teeth to make it
   look as if some were missing.
   The Brain invented a tooth remover machine.
   Binky Barnes offered to knock a tooth out with his fist.

2. Give each student a worksheet to make a list of suggestions
   they would have offered Arthur.

   Tie your tooth to the top of the Empire State Building and jump off.
   Chew ten packs of gum.
   Wear a mask.

Taking It Further . . .

Divide students into several groups of 4-6 children and then
invite them to write scripts for the movie, "Nasty Mr. Tooth
Decay." Before beginning to write, encourage students to do
some research on tooth decay causes and consequences.

Tooth Trouble

Arthur is the only one in his class who has never lost a tooth. Make a list of suggestions that might help Arthur lose his first tooth.

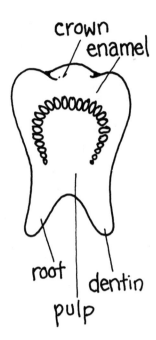

❧ • DENTAL HEALTH • ❧

Materials:

- 18" x 24" construction paper or poster board
- crayons or markers
- pencils

Lesson Procedure

1. On a sheet of poster board, draw one of Arthur's teeth and label the parts.
2. On another poster, draw all 32 teeth Arthur will have as an adult and label them.
3. Discuss the two posters with students.
4. Give each student a sheet of construction paper or poster board to design a dental health poster. Topics might include ways to prevent tooth decay, healthy snacks, types of tooth disease, or proper brushing methods.

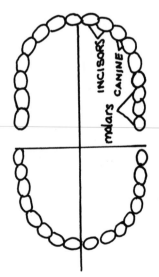

Taking It Further . . .

Arthur is an aardvark. In reality, aardvarks are toothless animals (edentate). Have students do research to find out some other interesting facts about aardvarks.

Arthur's Tooth

Arthur's

Arthur is embarrassed by some mysterious valentines sent to him from a secret admirer. All the fun and mischief of Valentine's Day comes out as Arthur deals with his misery and eventually finds a way to turn the tables on the culprit.

Boston: Little, Brown, 1980

Valentine

QUOTATION MARKS

Materials:

- candy conversation hearts
- lined paper
- pencils

Lesson Procedure

1. After reading the story, point out the conversation hearts on the endpapers of the book.
2. Give each student 6-10 candy conversation hearts. Invite students to read the messages on each heart and share some aloud with the class.
3. Discuss the proper use of quotation marks. Explain to students that quotation marks are like frames put around what someone is saying. Explain to students that they will be writing conversations using the words on their candy hearts. Provide some examples.

   When Superman met Superwoman he said, "Great!"
   Superwoman said, "Get lost."
   When mother told him to take out the garbage, Henry said, "Fine."

4. After students have written a sentence using the words on each heart, they can eat their candy.

Taking It Further . . .

Have students use the conversation hearts to answer each other's questions. For example, one student might ask, "What do you say when your mom or dad tells you to go to bed?" Another child can read a candy heart message, such as "Sure thing!"

· MATH COMPUTATION ·

Materials:

- •worksheet on page 48
- •pencils
- •crayons or markers

Lesson Procedure

1. Write an addition, subtraction, multiplication, or division problem on half of the hearts on the worksheet. Write the answers to each problem on the other half. Be sure that no two math problems have the same answer.
2. Duplicate the worksheet and give one to each student.
3. Students can match each math problem heart with the heart that has the correct answer. Then they can color the two hearts the same color. When the worksheet is completed, each heart will be colored and have a matching partner.

Taking It Further . . .

Write math problems on large cards cut into heart shapes. Hold up each heart-shaped flash card one at a time. The first student who can raise his or her hand and correctly answer the math problem receives a candy heart.

Heart Match

Color each heart with a math problem on it the same color as the
heart with the correct answer.

Arthur's Valentine

The Marc Brown Connection © 1991 Fearon Teacher Aids

ART SCAVENGER HUNT

Materials:

- black markers
- old magazines

Lesson Procedure

1. Encourage students to look around the room and find circles, rectangles, squares, or triangles in the objects, people, or pictures they see.
2. Ask students if they see any heart shapes around them.
3. Have students look through magazines for heart shapes and trace the shapes with a black marker. Suggest that they pay particular attention to faces and landscape pictures.
4. Have the students cut out the shapes. Arrange the children's shapes on a bulletin board in a heart-shaped configuration. This activity will help students observe their surroundings more analytically.

Taking It Further . . .

Divide students into several groups of 4-6 to study art prints or pictures in children's literature. Discuss how the artists have used different shapes.

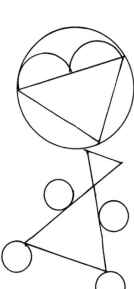

❧ • PAPER CHAINS • ❧

Materials:

•worksheet on page 51
•scissors

Lesson Procedure

1. Duplicate the worksheet on pink or red construction paper.
2. Give each student several copies of the worksheet.
3. Have students fold the worksheet in half on the dotted line.
4. Ask students to cut out the folded hearts, including the centers. Caution students not to cut on the folded edge.
5. Make a chain by lacing the folded hearts through each other.

Taking It Further . . .

Invite students to make paper chains using other shapes. The shapes must be folded and have a cut-out center. And, the folded end must be narrow.

fold

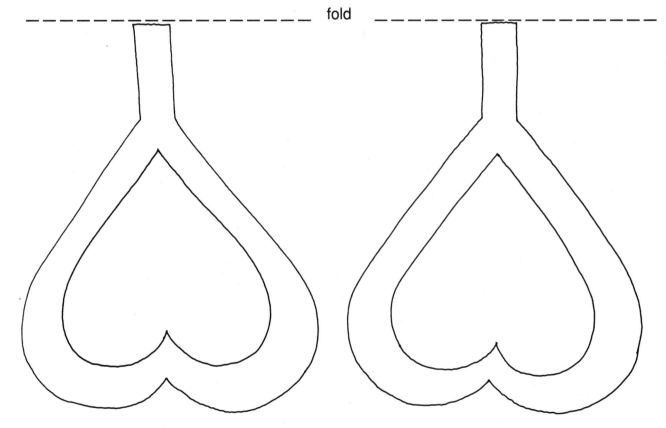

The Bionic

What really goes on behind the scenes in super character shows? Who is the real Bionic Bunny? Marc and Laurene Krasny Brown create a lot of laughs, while showing what goes into the making of a television show.

Written by Marc Brown and Laurene Krasny Brown

Boston: Little, Brown, 1984

Bunny Show

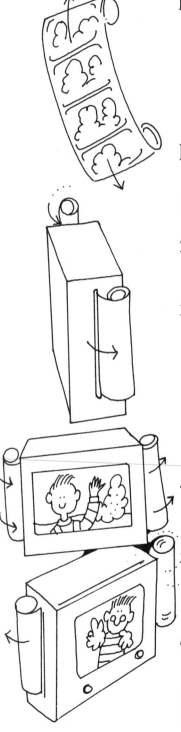

❧• CREATIVE WRITING •❧

Materials:

•worksheet on page 55
•lined paper
•pencils

Lesson Procedure

1. Discuss the television words and their meanings on the last page of the story.
2. Show children the endpapers of the book where the whole Bionic Bunny adventure is put together in sequence using comic-strip form.
3. Discuss the elements of a good Bionic Bunny episode.

   Actors—characters should include a hero (the Bionic Bunny) and villains
   Script—a good beginning, an action-filled middle, and an exciting ending
   Set—an appropriate background for the story
   Editing—changing, adjusting, deleting, and adding to original ideas and dialogue to make the story move smoothly

4. Have each student use a sheet of lined paper to plan characters, a crime, action scenes, an exotic setting, and a final solution for a Bionic Bunny episode.
5. After the plans have been made, give each student several copies of the worksheet to write and illustrate their cartoon episodes.

Taking It Further . . .

Students can make "television sets" using tissue boxes or shoeboxes. The stories that have been written and illustrated on the worksheets can be cut into strips and taped together. Glue the ends of the story strips to rollers made from paper towel cores.

Name _____

The Bionic Bunny Show

Can You Jump

Animals jump and fly across the pages of this pop-up book and invite readers to do the same. Small children will be charmed by the movement and older children will be intrigued by the mechanics of the book.

New York: E.P. Dutton, 1989

Like a Frog?

❧ • POP-UP BOOKS • ❧

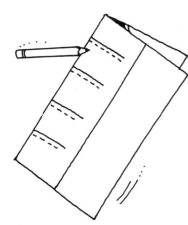

Materials:

- 8 ¹/₂" x 11" drawing paper
- pencils
- rulers
- scissors
- glue
- crayons or markers

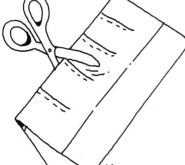

Lesson Procedure

1. Invite children to choose a favorite poem, fairy tale, or original story to illustrate with pop-up pages.
2. For each page, ask children to fold a sheet of drawing paper in half, measure 2 ¹/₂" from the folded edge, and draw a line.
3. Have children cut 4 slits on the folded edge, stopping short of the line they drew. Each pair of slits should be the same length to create the sides of what will be a pop-out box.
4. Reverse-fold the boxes.
5. Children can illustrate each page and add text. Invite children to draw or glue important characters or props on the pop-up boxes.
6. The pages can be glued back-to-back to create a complete pop-up book.

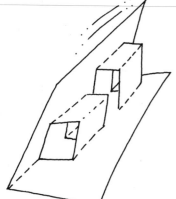

Taking It Further . . .

Students can experiment with the mechanics of making other moving parts or designing an intriguing cover for their pop-up books.

Can You Jump Like a Frog?

Dinosaurs,

Zany dinosaurs offer safety tips to show what to do in the event of an emergency. Other safety advice is given to prevent emergencies from happening. Obeying traffic lights, wearing seat belts, and keeping toys off the stairs can mean the difference between being safe or sorry.

Written by Marc Brown and
Steven Krensky
Boston: Little, Brown, 1982

Beware!

Materials:

- lined paper
- drawing paper
- pencils
- crayons, markers, or colored pencils

Lesson Procedure

1. For best results, read the story to children in small groups of 4-6. After everyone has had an opportunity to enjoy the book, discuss the categories of safety presented in the story. Ask children to recall the categories and make a list on the chalkboard.

At Home	With Animals	In the Car	In Cold Weather
In the Yard	On Wheels	At the Beach	At Night
During Meals	At the Playground	On Short Trips	
In Case of Fire	When Camping	Giving First Aid	

2. Make another list on the chalkboard of new categories not covered in the story.

In the Classroom	In the Cafeteria	On the Bus
In the Restroom	In the Hall	While Playing Sports

3. Divide students into several groups of 4-6. Invite each group to select a category and write appropriate safety rules. Each student in the group can illustrate one rule.
4. Compile all the safety rules into a class booklet.

Taking It Further . . .

Use the safety categories in *Dinosaurs, Beware!* to study dinosaurs.

At Home—Where did dinosaurs live?
In the Yard—Describe their environment.
During Meals—What did dinosaurs eat?
In Case of Fire—What natural disasters threatened dinosaurs?

Dinosaurs

An authoritative resource for children dealing with all aspects of divorce. The subject is handled with simplicity, humor, and sensitivity.

Written by Laurene Krasny Brown
and Marc Brown
Boston: Little, Brown, 1986

Divorce

CREATIVE WRITING

Materials:

•worksheet on page 63
•pencils

Lesson Procedure

1. After reading the entire story, reread the section entitled "Visiting Your Parent." Discuss what the author has to say about not needing to do things that are "fancy or expensive."
2. Students can use the worksheet to make a list of inexpensive things they would enjoy doing. Children who have divorced parents can make a list of things they would like to do with one of their parents. Other students can make a list of things they would like to do with a friend or relative that they don't see very often.
3. Encourage students to think about how to make the very best use of the time they have to spend with the parent, friend, or relative. Remind students of the author's statement, "You don't have to spend lots of money to love each other and have fun together."

Taking It Further . . .

Discuss how Marc Brown and his wife used dinosaurs to deal with serious problems. Suggest that students make a class booklet entitled, "Dinosaurs in School." Divide students into groups of 4-6 to identify problems in the classroom and suggest solutions. Each group can design a page to contribute to the class booklet.

Dinosaurs Divorce

Dinosaurs

Dinosaurs demonstrate helpful hints for travelers in this catalog of trains, planes, and subways. Children will enjoy the simple text and imaginative pictures whether they are planning a trip around the world or around the block.

Written by Laurene Krasny Brown
and Marc Brown
Boston: Little, Brown, 1988

Travel

✈ • ESTIMATION •

Materials:

- •worksheet on page 67
- •pencils
- •maps
- •rulers
- •newspaper travel sections, travel magazines, travel brochures, and sample menus

Lesson Procedure

1. Explain to students that they will be planning a one-week trip to anywhere in the world. They will plan mileage, expenses, and an itinerary.
2. Give each student a worksheet to record their plans as they research and calculate.
3. Invite students to look through the travel brochures to choose some exciting places to travel.
4. Using maps and rulers, students calculate the distance to and from their chosen destinations.
5. Using travel magazines and newspaper ads, have students estimate the cost of staying in a hotel for seven nights.
6. Using menus, ask students to estimate how much they would spend on meals for one week.
7. Students can make a seven-day calendar showing what they would like to see and do each day of their trip.

Taking It Further . . .

Encourage students to call an airline or travel agent for information on how long a flight to their destination would take. Students can calculate the time they would arrive, taking into consideration time zone changes.

Name _____

Planning a Trip

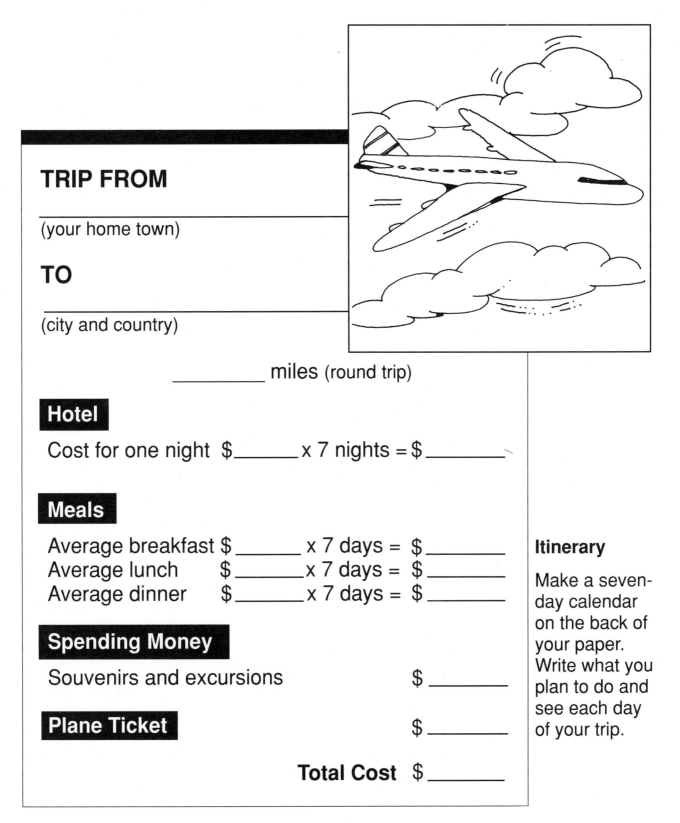

TRIP FROM

_____
(your home town)

TO

_____
(city and country)

_____ miles (round trip)

Hotel

Cost for one night $_____ x 7 nights = $_____

Meals

Average breakfast $_____ x 7 days = $_____
Average lunch $_____ x 7 days = $_____
Average dinner $_____ x 7 days = $_____

Spending Money

Souvenirs and excursions $_____

Plane Ticket $_____

Total Cost $_____

Itinerary

Make a seven-day calendar on the back of your paper. Write what you plan to do and see each day of your trip.

❧ • MAP SKILLS • ❧

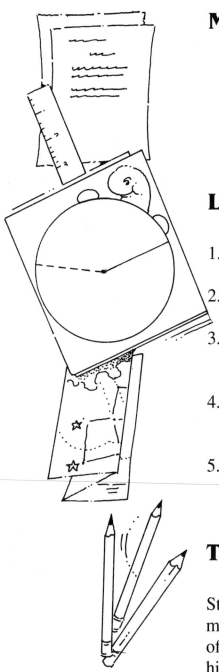

Materials:

- •worksheet on page 69
- •rulers
- •pencils
- •local maps

Lesson Procedure

1. Have students write the name of the city or town where they live on the line inside the circle on their worksheets.
2. Distribute maps and have students locate their city on the map.
3. Have students use the map scale and a ruler to determine a radius of 100 miles from their homes. Have students also write the number 100 in the blank on the worksheet.
4. Students can write the names of cities, towns, or points of interest that fall within the 100-mile radius in the circle on the worksheet.
5. The activity can also be done using a larger or smaller radius limit.

Taking It Further . . .

Students can choose another city anywhere in the world and make a radius map showing areas of interest near that city. Areas of interest might include other cities, rivers, lakes, parks, and historical points of interest.

Radius Map

Write the name of the city or town where you live on the line inside the circle. Fill in the blank with the number of miles your radius map will include. Use a map to fill the circle with names of cities, rivers, lakes, and points of interest that fall within your radius limit.

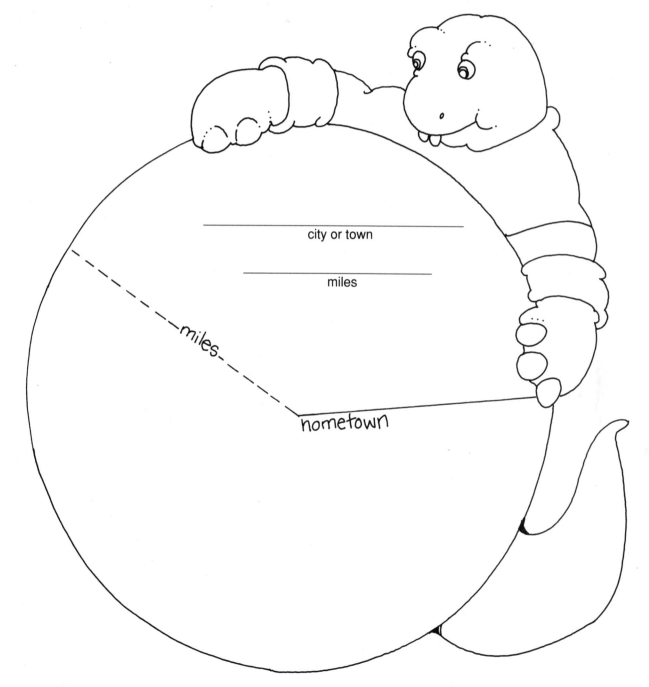

_____
city or town

_____
miles

miles

hometown

D.W.

It's the family's first day at the beach and D.W. insists that she does not intend to go near the water. With a little help from Arthur, D.W. discovers the joys of floating, flipping, squirting, and splashing in the ocean.

Boston: Little, Brown, 1988

All Wet

Materials:

   • worksheet on page 73
   • crayons or markers

Lesson Procedure

1. Explain to students that they will be designing new swimsuits for Arthur and D.W.
2. Discuss use of color and design (stripes, spots, patterns).
3. Invite students to use crayons or markers to draw the swimsuits on the worksheet.
4. Display the swimsuit creations on a bulletin board.

Taking It Further . . .

Students can write advertising copy for their swimsuit creations. Encourage them to use descriptive and persuasive words.

Designer Swimsuits

D.W. All Wet

❧ • SAND SCULPTURES • ❧

Materials:

- •sandbox
- •sand
- •water
- •assorted cups and buckets

Lesson Procedure

1. After reading the story, flip back through the book and point out the illustrations of the sand castles D.W. made.
2. Invite children to take turns working individually or in small groups to create original sand castles using the materials provided in a sandbox.

Taking It Further . . .

Students can draw sand castles on drawing paper. Have students spread thinned white glue over their pictures and then sprinkle sand on the glue area. Have students shake the excess sand off the picture into a bucket. Let the sand castle pictures dry and then details can be added with crayons or markers.

D.W.

D.W. thinks she is ready for complicated acrobatics when she enters her gymnastics class on the first day. However, D.W. cannot manage even a simple forward roll. Children will identify with the humor and agony of D.W.'s struggle to accomplish a new task.

Boston: Little, Brown, 1987

Flips

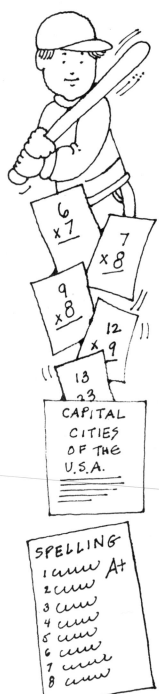

PERSONAL ACHIEVEMENT

Materials:

•lined paper
•pencils

Lesson Procedure

1. Ask students to tell about recreation or art classes they have taken and the experiences they most remember.
2. Discuss what other classes D.W. might consider enrolling in after completing her gymnastics class. List suggestions on the chalkboard.

   dancing
   swimming
   piano

3. Invite students to select a class for D.W. to enroll in and then write a story describing her expectations, frustrations, and accomplishments.

Taking It Further . . .

Discuss goal setting with students. Encourage students to think of some personal goals they would like to accomplish. Invite students to write down their goals and seal them in an envelope. A month later, have students open the envelopes and check their progress.

   hit a home run
   get an A in spelling
   do ten push-ups
   learn multiplication facts
   memorize the capital cities of all 50 states

Finger

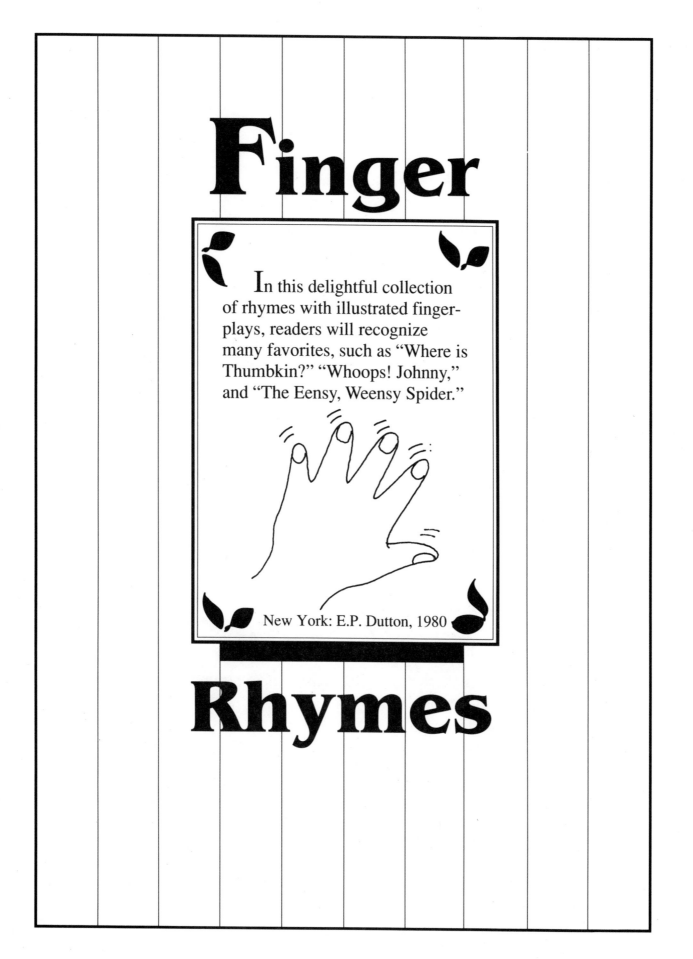

In this delightful collection of rhymes with illustrated finger-plays, readers will recognize many favorites, such as "Where is Thumbkin?" "Whoops! Johnny," and "The Eensy, Weensy Spider."

New York: E.P. Dutton, 1980

Rhymes

❦ • CLASSROOM MANAGEMENT • ❧

Materials:

Lesson Procedure

1. Read several of the rhymes from the book and teach children how to do the fingerplays that go with them.
2. Discuss ways we use our fingers and hands to communicate with others.

   One curling finger means "come here."
   Arm extended with palm facing out means "stop."
   Two fingers means "victory" or "peace."
   Thumbs up means "good going!"

3. Review your classroom rules. Invite students to create hand or finger signs for each rule.

   Finger by lips means "no talking."
   Two fingers "walking" on your arm means "walk."
   Closed palm means "respect property."

4. Use these non-verbal messages to remind students of proper classroom behavior.

Taking It Further . . .

Students can play a game of charades by acting out incidents that have happened on the playground or in the classroom. Other students can try to guess which situations are being silently described.

One, Two,

This charming book will delight preschoolers with its lively illustrations. It will intrigue older children with its inventive pop-up design. It will captivate readers of all ages with its rhythmical revival of the traditional counting rhyme.

New York: E.P. Dutton, 1989

Buckle My Shoe

❦ · WRITING COUPLETS · ❧

Materials:

• lined paper
• pencils

Lesson Procedure

1. Discuss the rhyming couplets in the book and point out the position of the rhyming words in each line.

> One, two,
> buckle my shoe.
> Three, four,
> knock at the door.

2. Encourage students to experiment with variations of these couplets and write their ideas on the chalkboard.

> One, two,
> my nose is blue.

3. Invite students to use animal names or letter names to begin their rhyming couplets.

> Bear, bear
> with purple hair.
> A, B,
> drink some tea.

4. Encourage creativity as students write their own original rhyming couplets.

Taking It Further . . .

Invite students to make note cards by folding a small piece of construction paper in half and writing the first line of the couplet on the outside of the note card and the second line on the inside. Students can illustrate the cards as well. A set of six note cards and envelopes makes a nice gift for parents, relatives, or friends.

One Two

Alive with creativity, pattern, and design, this counting book is filled with characters and hidden numbers. Children will enjoy Marc Brown's playfulness.

Boston: Little, Brown, 1976

Three

❧ • NUMBER DAYS • ❧

Materials:

- •drawing paper
- •pencils
- •crayons or markers

Lesson Procedure

1. Plan to celebrate one of the numbers from one to ten each day of the week.
2. On each celebration day, students can bring from home a number of objects to correspond to the number for that day. For example, on "One Day," each student can bring one special object from home. On "Seven Day," students can bring seven identical objects (marbles, clips, stamps).
3. On each celebration day, have students draw their objects on a sheet of drawing paper and label them. Save the pages from each day to make a counting booklet.

Taking It Further . . .

Students can design a fancy, ornate numeral of the day. Draw a large block numeral for each child. Invite students to fill in the numeral with collage materials or patterns made with crayons or markers.

Party

Favorite illustrated rhyming songs, including "The Farmer in the Dell," "Pawpaw Patch," "Skip to My Lou," and "The Muffin Man," are presented with melody lines and directions for creative movement.

New York: E.P. Dutton, 1988

Rhymes

❧ · SEQUENCING · ❧

Materials:

- drawing paper
- crayons or markers

Lesson Procedure

1. After reading "The Farmer in the Dell," ask students to name all the characters in the song and list them on the chalkboard.

farmer	nurse	rat
wife	dog	cheese
child	cat	

2. Write each character's name on a sheet of drawing paper. Choose one student to hold each character's name.
3. Students holding the names stand in front of the room in mixed-up order. Call on other student volunteers to put the characters in order according to the sequence of the song.
4. Repeat the activity with "She'll Be Coming Round the Mountain." Have students act out the parts by doing appropriate motions rather than holding name cards.

Taking It Further . . .

Students can select a rhyme and illustrate it on 3" x 5" cards. Encourage children to scramble the cards and then have a partner put them in sequential order.

Perfect

This delightful book of manners addresses proper behavior during meals, while on the telephone, at school, and for many other occasions and situations. The silly pig illustrations bring these manner reminders to life in a humorous way.

Written by Marc Brown and
Stephen Krensky
Boston: Little, Brown, 1983

Pigs

PIG ART

Materials:

- •worksheet on page 87
- •drawing paper
- •pencils
- •crayons or markers

Lesson Procedure

1. Give each child a worksheet and point out the step-by-step sequence showing how to draw a simple pig.
2. Encourage children to experiment drawing the pig on the bottom of the worksheet.
3. Once children have practiced the technique, encourage them to draw some pigs on a sheet of drawing paper and add their own special touches, such as accessories and facial expressions.

Taking It Further . . .

Set up a Pig Museum. Invite students to bring stuffed pigs, pig pictures, and other pig memorabilia from home. Students can label their exhibits with the title, artist, and a short description of the piece.

Draw a Pig

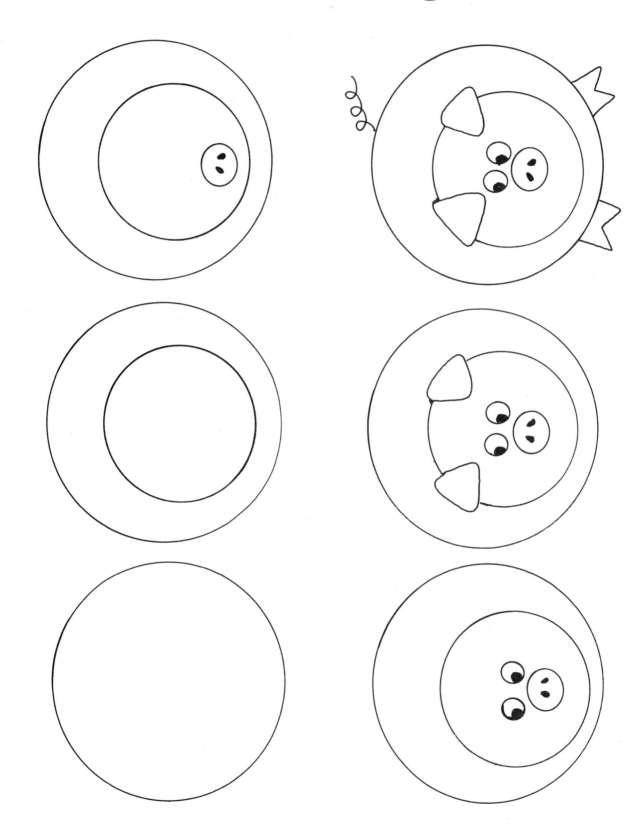

❦ • GRAMMAR • ❦

Materials:

• lined paper
• drawing paper
• pencils

Lesson Procedure

1. Discuss the format of the book. Ask children to recall some of the section headings (With Your Family, On the Telephone, With Pets).
2. Ask for student ideas on how to make a "Perfect Pigs" book of language rules. List some section headings on the chalkboard that would be appropriate.

   punctuation   verb tense   paragraphs
   capitalization   plurals

3. Invite children individually or in small groups to select categories and write rules.
4. Encourage children to add funny pig illustrations (using the pig they learned how to draw from the lesson on page 87 or their own imaginations) to emphasize each rule with humor.

Taking It Further . . .

Combine all the pages into a class booklet entitled, "Perfect Pigs Book of Grammar Greats."

Play

With illustrated motions to provide participation for young children, this book includes such delightful poems as "The Crocodile," "Teddy Bear," "Wheels on the Bus," and "I'm a Little Teapot."

New York: E.P. Dutton, 1987

Rhymes

❖ • CREATIVE WRITING • ❖

Materials:

- lined paper
- pencils

Lesson Procedure

1. After reading several of the animal poems, discuss different ways that animals move.
2. Invite each child to choose an animal from the book or a favorite animal and write a poem about the way that animal moves.
3. Provide suggestions and examples to help children get started.

   Alliteration—Boas slink, slither, and slide.
   Repetition—The camel goes bump, bump, bump, with a load on his hump, hump, hump.
   Onomatopoeia—The whale swishes, swooshes, and sings, "Beep, squeak, beep."

Taking It Further . . .

Students can take turns reading their poems while others act out the movements. Find suitable music to play that conveys the proper feeling for specific animal movements. Children can also illustrate their poems.

The True

Francine is wrongfully accused of cheating on the big math test. Because of this accusation, she will miss the big softball game against Miss Sweetwater's class. Should she tell Mr. Ratburn the truth? This is a strong story of honesty and friendship.

Boston: Little, Brown, 1981

Francine

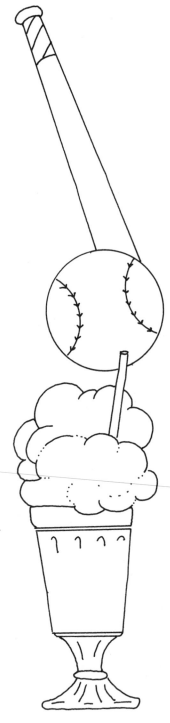

❧ • COMPREHENSION • ❧

Materials:

- lined paper
- pencils

Lesson Procedure

1. After reading the story, ask students to recall word and picture clues to help contribute to a character sketch of Mr. Ratburn.

   Students do not want him for a teacher. (Anyone's better than Mr. Ratburn.)

   He did not allow students to choose their own seats. (In Mr. Ratburn's class, everyone sat in alphabetical order.)

   He made the students memorize a lot of facts. (Mr. Ratburn had the state capitals written on the chalkboard.)

   Maybe he had been to Hawaii. (He wore a tie that had the word "Aloha" printed on it.)

   He didn't always treat students fairly. (He punished Francine for something Muffy had done.)

   He made his class do difficult math problems. (There were 6-digit math problems written on the chalkboard.)

   Sometimes he was nice. (He treated everyone to sodas.)

2. Encourage students to use word and picture clues to write a personality sketch about another character in the book.

Taking It Further . . .

Have a Mr. Ratburn Day. In the morning, students do Ratburn Math (big problems), memorize state capitals, and write turtle reports. In the afternoon, children can have a big softball game and perhaps end the day enjoying sodas.

ADDITION

Materials:

- •worksheet on page 94
- •pencils
- •dice

Lesson Procedure

1. Francine suggested that Muffy play "scorekeeper." She reminded Muffy that she would have to learn to add. Explain to the students that they will be practicing scorekeeping.
2. Give each child a copy of the worksheet. Invite children to work in pairs and give each pair of children a die.
3. Have children roll the die and write the number in the first score box to represent the runs Mr. Ratburn's team scored in the first inning. Children continue rolling the die until the score boxes for each inning for both teams are filled.
4. Have students practice their addition skills by totaling the runs for each team in all three games.

Taking It Further . . .

Students can have fun figuring imaginary batting averages for team members on both teams. Give the students a number representing the number of hits made by a player and tell them the number of times the player was at bat. Students can use their math skills to divide the number of hits by the number of times at bat and round to three decimal places. For example, if a player made one hit and was at bat three times during a game, the player's batting average would be .333.

Scorekeeping

GAME ONE

INNINGS	1	2	3	4	5	6	7	8	9	T
RATBURN										
SWEETWATER										

GAME TWO

INNINGS	1	2	3	4	5	6	7	8	9	T
RATBURN										
SWEETWATER										

GAME THREE

INNINGS	1	2	3	4	5	6	7	8	9	T
RATBURN										
SWEETWATER										

Visiting the

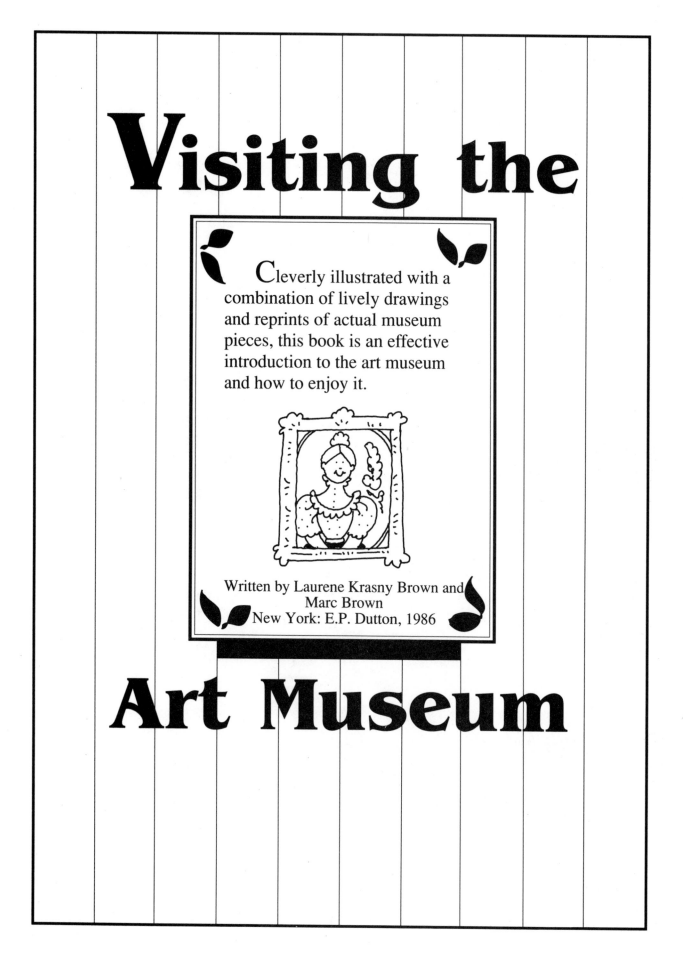

Cleverly illustrated with a combination of lively drawings and reprints of actual museum pieces, this book is an effective introduction to the art museum and how to enjoy it.

Written by Laurene Krasny Brown and Marc Brown
New York: E.P. Dutton, 1986

Art Museum

◀ • SCALE DRAWING • ▶

Materials:

- graph paper ($^1/4$")
- rulers
- pencils

Lesson Procedure

1. Remind children that the art pieces in the museum were displayed according to categories. Each room the family visited displayed works of art from a particular period of time. Expose children to the names of some of these periods of history by making a list on the chalkboard of the various galleries.

   Primitive Gallery   Renaissance Gallery   20th Century Abstract Art
   Ancient Egyptian Gallery   18th Century Gallery   20th Century Pop Art
   Classical Greek Gallery   Impressionist Gallery
   Arms and Armor Gallery   Post-Impressionist Gallery

2. Give each student a sheet of graph paper to design a floor plan for a museum.
3. Direct children to include four or five galleries and use a scale of $^1/4$ inch (one square on the graph paper) representing one foot. Floor plans should include a lobby and doors into each gallery.
4. After the plans are drawn, instruct children to write the dimensions of each room inside its interior.

Taking It Further . . .

Use the information in the back of *Visiting the Art Museum* to provide children with interesting details about each art piece. Share the "Tips for Enjoying an Art Museum" and then plan a field trip to put the information to use.

☙• ART APPRECIATION •❧

Materials:

•lined paper
•pencils
•art prints and facsimiles (optional)

Lesson Procedure

1. Provide your students with the opportunity to visit an art museum or create your own display of art prints and facsimiles in the classroom.
2. Invite students to make a list of 4-6 of their favorite exhibits or prints with a brief description of each one.
3. Make a list on the chalkboard of some of the characters in Marc Brown's books.

   Arthur
   Muffy
   Francine
   Buster
   The Brain
   Binky Barnes

4. Have students choose three characters and write comments about the art exhibits they chose from each character's point of view.

   "The Thinker" by Auguste Rodin

   Francine might say, "He's probably trying to remember where he left his clothes."
   Muffy might say, "I think he would look better in a good color-coordinated outfit."
   The Brain might say, "I bet he's thinking about a famous discovery."
   Binky Barnes might say, "I don't care what anybody says. With those muscles, I wouldn't mess with him."

Taking It Further . . .

Students can do the same activity using characters from other books they have read.

What Do You

Every page of this rabbit catalog is packed with hare-raising hilarity. There are riddles, jokes, puzzles, flip books, and many delightful surprises to intrigue young readers for hours.

Boston: Little, Brown, 1983

Call a Dumb Bunny?

❧ • PAPER FOLDING • ❧

Materials:

- 8 ¹/₂" x 11" drawing paper
- pencils
- scissors
- crayons or markers

Lesson Procedure

1. Cut the drawing paper in half lengthwise to make 4 ¹/₄" x 11" strips. Give each child one of the paper strips.
2. Have children fold the strip of paper in half twice to make four sections.
3. Invite children to draw a simple rabbit shape on the top section of the folded strip. Caution children to be sure the front and back legs of the rabbit touch the folded sides. (Provide a rabbit pattern for smaller children to trace onto their folded strips.)
4. Children can cut out the rabbit shape and then unfold the paper strip. (The folded sides where the front and back legs touch are not to be cut. If the entire outline of the rabbit is cut around, the rabbits will not be connected when the strip is unfolded.)
5. Encourage children to color and add details to each rabbit using crayons or markers.

Taking It Further . . .

On the back of each rabbit, students can write poetic couplets or rabbit facts.

What Do You Call a Dumb Bunny?

Your First

This how-to book is filled with useful information, experiments, and projects. Marc Brown has drawn from his personal experience as a "gentleman farmer" to create a book that takes the fear out of gardening.

Boston: Little, Brown, 1981

Garden Book

FANTASY FLOWERS

Materials:

- 12" x 18" drawing paper
- pencils
- fine-tip markers or colored pencils

Lesson Procedure

1. Discuss the parts of a flower:

   blossom   leaf
   stem   roots

2. Invite students to draw "fantasy flowers" with intricate detailing. Encourage curlicues, patterns, and branching lines.
3. Have students label the parts of the flower when the drawing is complete.

Taking It Further . . .

Students can write paragraphs about their unique plants. Encourage them to explain in what part of the world their plant would grow, what its special needs and beneficial attributes are.

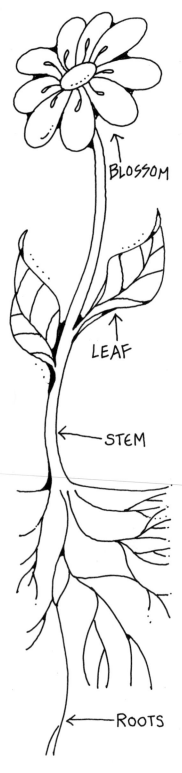

BLOSSOM

LEAF

STEM

ROOTS

DUE DATE